P9-CAY-198

SNAPSHOTS IN HISTORY

THE MARCH ON WASHINGTON

Uniting Against Racism

by Robin S. Doak

THE MARCH ON WASHINGTON

Uniting Against Racism

by Robin S. Doak

Content Adviser: Stephen Asperheim, Ph.D.,
Assistant Professor of History, Savannah State University

Reading Adviser: Katie Van Sluys, Ph.D.,
School of Education, DePaul University

Compass Point Books ✦ Minneapolis, Minnesota

✦ COMPASS POINT BOOKS

3109 West 50th Street, #115
Minneapolis, MN 55410

Visit Compass Point Books on the Internet at
www.compasspointbooks.com
or e-mail your request to
custserv@compasspointbooks.com

For Compass Point Books
Jennifer VanVoorst, Jaime Martens, Lori Bye, XNR Productions, Inc.,
Catherine Neitge, Keith Griffin, and Nick Healy

Produced by White-Thomson Publishing Ltd.

For White-Thomson Publishing
Stephen White-Thomson, Susan Crean, Amy Sparks,
Tinstar Design Ltd., Stephen Asperheim, Peggy Bresnick Kendler,
Brian Fitzgerald, Barbara Bakowski, and Timothy Griffin

Library of Congress Cataloging-in-Publication Data
Doak, Robin S. (Robin Santos), 1963–
    The March on Washington : Uniting Against Racism / by Robin S. Doak.
        p. cm. — (Snapshots in history)
    ISBN-13: 978-0-7565-3339-7 (library binding)
    ISBN-10: 0-7565-3339-2 (library binding)
1. March on Washington for Jobs and Freedom, Washington, D.C.,
1963—Juvenile literature. 2. Civil rights demonstrations—Washington
(D.C.)—History—20th century—Juvenile literature. 3. African
Americans—Civil rights—History—20th century—Juvenile literature. I.
Title.
    F200.D63 2007
    323.1196'073009046—dc22   2007004918

CONTENTS

Sharing a Dream

Chapter

1

On the afternoon of August 28, 1963, Martin Luther King Jr. stood silently behind the speaker's podium in Washington, D.C. Behind him, the marble statue of Abraham Lincoln gazed out over the National Mall. In front of him, an audience of 250,000 people stood restlessly in the hot summer sun, waiting for the civil rights leader to speak.

Over the past few days, these thousands of people from all walks of life had traveled across the nation and around the world to be part of the March on Washington for Jobs and Freedom. Some had traveled in groups, while others came alone to the nation's capital. They arrived on buses, trains, cars, and planes. Some spent their last pennies to get to Washington, D.C. Some people hitchhiked, and others walked. One man

Martin Luther King Jr. was one of the last speakers to address the hot and tired crowd on August 28, 1963.

roller-skated hundreds of miles to be part of the March on Washington.

For many black Americans, especially those living in the South, attending the march was an act of bravery. In the struggle for civil rights, the summer of 1963 had been one of the nation's most violent. Black and white people taking part in peaceful civil rights protests had been beaten with police clubs. They had been knocked down in the streets by powerful streams from fire hoses and had police dogs turned loose on them. Many had been arrested for doing nothing more than quietly asserting that African-Americans deserved to be treated equally.

Marchers arrived in Washington, D.C.'s Union Station early on the morning of the march.

Many people throughout the nation believed that the March on Washington would end up being a violent, bloody event. Police, military, and government officials had prepared for rioting. Yet despite these fears, hundreds of thousands of people from all walks of life chose to travel to Washington, D.C. They wanted to send a clear, strong message: The U.S. government must pass laws to protect African-Americans from discrimination, segregation, and violence. The marchers believed that racism was wrong, and they had come to Washington to demand that the government do something about it. They also wanted to hear Martin Luther King Jr., a man who had just been introduced to the audience of one-quarter of a million people.

King, a Baptist minister from Montgomery, Alabama, was used to addressing his congregation each Sunday, but never before had he spoken to such a large crowd. He knew that as a leader of the civil rights movement, his words on this day would be important. The night before the march, King had spent hours perfecting his speech, carefully examining every word he would say. He knew the world would be listening.

CIVIL RIGHTS LEADER

Martin Luther King Jr. was born in Atlanta, Georgia, on January 15, 1929. A gifted student, King was accepted at Atlanta's Morehouse College when he was just 15 years old. There he joined a civil rights group and began working for fair treatment for African-Americans in the United States. King moved to Montgomery, Alabama, in 1954 to take a position as a Baptist minister. Ten years and many struggles later, he was awarded the Nobel Peace Prize for his civil rights work.

When King began speaking, his voice was steady and deliberate. He talked about the promise of freedom the Emancipation Proclamation had held out to slaves during the Civil War. Then he said:

> *But one hundred years later, the Negro still is not free. One hundred years later, the life of the Negro is still sadly crippled by the manacles [handcuffs] of segregation and the chains of discrimination. One hundred years later, the Negro lives on a lonely island of poverty in the midst of a vast ocean of material prosperity. One hundred years later, the Negro is still languished in the corners of American society and finds himself an exile in his own land.*

As King continued speaking, the audience cheered and applauded his words. Then, as he neared the end of his speech, gospel singer Mahalia Jackson, seated behind him, called out, "Tell them about the dream, Martin!"

King paused. When he spoke again, his voice rang out loud and strong, He said:

> *I have a dream that one day this nation will rise up and live out the true meaning of its creed: 'We hold these truths to be self-evident, that all men are created equal.' I have a dream that one day on the red hills of Georgia, the sons of former slaves and the sons of former slave owners will be able to sit down together at the table of brotherhood.*

As King's words sank in, the people in the audience forgot about the heat and crowds. Some cried as they listened to his words. Others clasped the hand of the person standing next to them. Many shouted their approval and applauded. King continued:

I have a dream that my four little children will one day live in a nation where they will not be judged by the color of their skin but by the content of their character. I have a dream today!

Nearly one-quarter of a million people heard King deliver his famous speech in person; millions of others listened to him on radios or televisions.

13

Millions of Americans who did not attend the march watched and listened to the speech. All of the major television networks had interrupted their regular programs to broadcast King's speech live. They had seen the huge crowd cheer and applaud King as he was introduced. Now Americans listened as King finished his historic speech:

When we allow freedom ring, when we let it ring from every village and every hamlet, from every state and every city, we will be able to speed up that day when all of God's children— black men and white men, Jews and Gentiles, Protestants and Catholics—will be able to join hands and sing in the words of the old Negro spiritual, 'Free at last! Free at last! Thank God Almighty, we are free at last!'

Thousands of marchers, both black and white, gathered on the National Mall to hear King and other civil rights leaders speak.

King's speech was the highlight of the March on Washington for Jobs and Freedom. The speech would later be remembered as one of the greatest in history. It helped energize and motivate many civil rights workers. It also placed King firmly at the head of the civil rights movement. And many believe that it helped ensure the passage of federal laws to end segregation.

The March on Washington had a huge impact on Americans. People across the nation were awakened to the racism that still existed in parts of the United States. Civil rights leader John Lewis, who also spoke at the march, said:

> *For the first time in people's living room[s] they saw, they heard, they could almost feel and touch what the movement was all about.*

Americans were equally impressed by the marchers, who were peaceful yet determined to bring about change. The March on Washington proved that the civil rights movement could not be ignored. After 100 years, black Americans were demanding to be truly free. ◣

Separate but Not Equal

Chapter

2

Beginning in the early 1600s, nearly 400,000 people were kidnapped from Africa and brought to the colonies that would one day be the United States. They were then sold as slaves. For the next 250 years, most of the descendants of these first African-Americans remained enslaved. White owners looked upon these enslaved people as property and often treated them no better than animals. These attitudes and behaviors continued in many areas of the United States into the 1800s.

In 1863, a century before the March on Washington, the United States was being torn apart by the Civil War, the bloodiest conflict in American history. The war began in 1861, when Southern states broke away from the rest of the nation to form the Confederate States of America. Two years after the fighting started, President Abraham Lincoln issued the Emancipation Proclamation. This historic document freed all slaves in the states that were in rebellion against the Union. It marked the beginning of the end of slavery in the United States.

Slavery officially ended after the Civil War with the passage of the 13th Amendment to the U.S. Constitution. With the 13th Amendment, thousands of slaves were freed. But for most African-Americans, equality and fair treatment did not come with freedom from slavery.

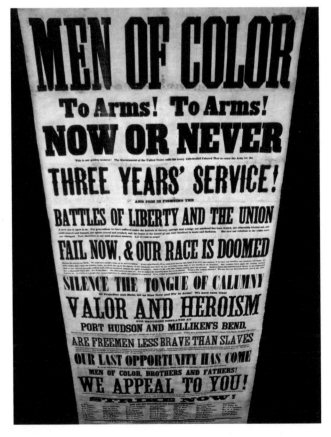

During the Civil War, African-Americans were urged to join the Army to fight the Confederacy.

In many states, particularly those in the South, African-American citizens were not given the same rights as white citizens. Southern states often used Jim Crow laws to make sure that African-Americans remained segregated from white people in public places. African-American children attended separate, inferior schools, while their parents were forced to use water fountains, waiting rooms, restaurants, movie theaters, and restrooms that were separate from those used by white people. The facilities for African-Americans often were dirty, run-down, and substandard compared to those used by white people.

African-American men and women who spoke out against this unfair system risked their lives. From 1882 to 1963, a total of 3,444 African-Americans were lynched, or killed by a mob. African-Americans were beaten and tortured for real or imagined

WHO WAS JIM CROW?

Jim Crow laws were rules and regulations that legalized the segregation of whites and blacks throughout the South. The laws were named for a character that was common in minstrel shows. In these musical shows, white actors would blacken their faces with burnt cork or other makeup and "imitate" black people. The shows reinforced stereotypes and prejudices against African-Americans that were already present throughout the United States. The Jim Crow character was introduced in 1828 by a white actor named Thomas Dartmouth Rice, known as the "Father of the American Minstrel." Jim Crow was a buffoon, a dancing and singing clown who wore tattered clothes. The character was wildly successful and helped popularize minstrel shows throughout the nation. In time, the phrase "Jim Crow" became an insulting name for black people, and Jim Crow laws became another way to deprive blacks of their rights.

crimes they had committed. Such "crimes" might have included attempting to vote, talking back to a white man, or insulting a white woman. One black man was even lynched for being unpopular. Violent executions and beatings of black citizens occurred throughout the nation, not just in the South. And these crimes usually went unpunished.

Although it was less obvious, racism existed in the North, too. Blacks there often faced discrimination in housing and employment. They were forced to live in the poorest, most run-down sections of cities because realtors refused to sell them houses or bankers refused to give them home loans. They were given the most menial jobs or were paid less than white people for doing the same work.

In 1909, the first important group to agitate for equality for blacks was formed in the United States. The National Association for the Advancement of Colored People (NAACP) was founded in New York City by both blacks and whites to protest segregation and violence against Americans of African descent. The following year, the Committee on Urban Conditions Among Negroes was formed in New York City to aid impoverished blacks who had moved to the city from the South. A decade later, the group would change its name to the National Urban League.

Between 1910 and 1940, a few advances were made on the civil rights front. In 1915 and 1919, for example, important court decisions were handed down in an effort to equalize blacks' voting and legal rights with those of whites. In 1933, the NAACP began a strategy of pursuing equal rights through the U.S. court system.

The 1940s and 1950s marked a time of early civil rights activity on the national level. In 1941, civil rights leader A. Philip Randolph felt that President Franklin D. Roosevelt was not doing enough to help African-Americans. World War II was under way, and the U.S. economy was beginning to strengthen as factories churned out weapons, ammunition, and other items to sell to European countries at war. Thousands of white men, out of work since the Great Depression, now found jobs. But racist hiring policies in the defense industry kept black Americans from sharing in the boom.

Randolph called for 10,000 black men to march on Washington, D.C., in protest. He believed that such a show of outrage was the only way to fix the problem. He said:

> *Let no black man be afraid. We are simply fighting for our constitutional rights as American citizens. Let us not be beaten, bewildered, and bitter. ... This is our own, our native land. Let us fight to make it truly free, democratic, and just.*

With the help of his friend Bayard Rustin, Randolph planned the march for July 1, 1941.

Randolph then traveled throughout the South, encouraging black men to join the march. By early June, Randolph believed that as many as 100,000 people would show up for the event. Roosevelt called the civil rights leader to the White House and asked him to call off the march. Randolph refused. One week after the meeting, the president issued an order banning racist hiring practices in the defense industry. The march was canceled.

While Randolph was fighting for equality of workers, James Farmer and other students in Chicago, Illinois, were starting to fight against segregation. These young people founded the Congress of Racial Equality (CORE) in 1942. The group's goal was to use nonviolent means to end racism and discrimination in the United States.

Another important advance in the early civil rights movement took place in 1954, when the U.S. Supreme Court ordered states to integrate public schools. The court's decision, known as *Brown v. Board of Education,* infuriated segregationists. Senator James O. Eastland of Mississippi said:

> *Separation promotes racial harmony. ... Segregation is not discrimination. Segregation is not a badge of racial inferiority, and that it is not is recognized by both races in the Southern states.*

Many Southern states refused to obey the Supreme Court order to integrate public schools.

Others obeyed only when threatened with military action. In 1957, for example, the National Guard had to escort nine black students into Central High School in Little Rock, Arkansas, because they had been refused entry to the school. Other schools closed their doors altogether in order to avoid integration. By 1963, little progress had been made: Less than one-half of 1 percent of African-American children in the South were attending integrated public schools.

One year after *Brown v. Board of Education*, a 42-year-old seamstress in Montgomery, Alabama, decided to take a stand against segregation—by staying seated. On December 1, 1955, Rosa Parks refused to give up her seat on a bus to a white man. Parks' arrest for violating the city's segregation laws led to a boycott of the Montgomery bus system. For more than 12 months, black citizens walked,

THE MOTHER OF THE CIVIL RIGHTS MOVEMENT

Born in Alabama in 1913, Rosa Parks grew up with racism and segregation. As a child, she attended all-black schools and watched the Ku Klux Klan, a racist hate group, march in front of her home. As an adult, she joined the National Association for the Advancement of Colored People (NAACP), a group dedicated to fighting for civil rights. After her arrest for refusing to give up her seat, Parks refused to pay the $13 fine and was arrested again. On December 5, the day of her trial, the Montgomery bus boycott began. Parks was found guilty, fined $14, and given a suspended jail sentence. She is considered the mother of the civil rights movement.

carpooled, or used special taxis to travel to and from work. Eventually, the city agreed to desegregate public transportation. Today the Montgomery bus boycott is considered the start of the modern civil rights movement.

Rosa Parks took her first ride on a desegregated Montgomery public bus in December 1956. It was more than a year after she refused to give up her seat to a white man.

In the late 1950s and early 1960s, the battle for civil rights heated up. New groups were formed to fight for fair treatment. The Southern Christian Leadership Conference (SCLC), founded in 1957, had its roots in the Montgomery bus boycott of 1955–1956. This organization's original goal was to support other groups that worked for civil rights and to help arrange protests across the South. Martin Luther King Jr., who helped found the organization, served as its president until his death in April 1968.

Another group was the Student Nonviolent Coordinating Committee (SNCC), founded in 1960. SNCC was created by college students in Raleigh, North Carolina, who wanted to use nonviolent protest in their struggle for equal rights for African-Americans. SNCC joined with other established civil rights groups, such as CORE and the SCLC, to organize nonviolent protests.

One type of nonviolent protest popular with students was the sit-in. Black and white students would enter a segregated restaurant or public area and remain there until they were physically thrown out or arrested. Freedom Rides were another type of protest. On Freedom Rides, blacks and whites together rode on segregated interstate bus routes and sat together in segregated waiting areas. In May 1963, *The New York Times* estimated that 75,000 Americans had taken part in civil rights demonstrations during a one-month period.

Although the protesters practiced nonviolence, segregationists rarely did the same. At sit-ins, protesters were doused with ketchup, sugar, and any other items that were at hand. They were often slapped, punched, or spat on. Freedom Riders

Black and white students used sit-ins at white lunch counters to peacefully protest segregation and discrimination. Packages of napkins on nearby stools were meant to discourage other protesters from joining the sit-in.

risked being pulled from buses and beaten or killed. In some places, the buses were bombed.

In November 1960, Senator John F. Kennedy of Massachusetts was elected president by a small margin. During his campaign, Kennedy had promised to end segregation. Many black people felt that their votes for Kennedy had put him in the White House. Civil rights leaders were soon disappointed, however. Worried about upsetting Southern politicians, Kennedy at first did very little to advance civil rights or improve the lives of African-Americans.

By late 1962, A. Philip Randolph believed that the time had come to take definitive action. Born in Florida in 1889, Randolph had spent his entire life fighting for equal rights. In 1917, he founded a civil rights magazine. Eight years later, he organized the Brotherhood of Sleeping Car Porters, a union for African-American porters who waited on passengers, carried luggage, and cleaned sleeping cars on trains. The same year, he helped 10,000 black porters at the Pullman Company win a wage increase by threatening to go out on strike.

Randolph never gave up on his dream from 1941 of a mass protest in the nation's capital. Since then, he and Bayard Rustin had exchanged letters about organizing a march. Finally, in December 1962, the 73-year-old civil rights leader decided that it was time to try again. At this time, the unemployment rate for black people was twice as high as that for

A. Philip Randolph was an experienced civil rights activist who had successfully fought for black civil rights since before the 1940s.

whites. African-Americans who held jobs were consistently earning much less than their white co-workers. What the United States needed, Randolph decided, was a wake-up call, a reminder that African-Americans deserved equal treatment in the workplace.

The Big Six

Chapter

3

In late March 1963, Randolph began sending his proposal for a march for equality in the workplace to the most important civil rights groups around the nation. He hoped these groups would sponsor the march. At first, few people were interested in the idea. But in early May, events in Birmingham, Alabama, changed that.

In the 1950s and early 1960s, Birmingham was one of the most segregated cities in the country. The city's police commissioner, T. Eugene "Bull" Connor, had become a symbol of white racism. He often ordered his officers to break up black political meetings, and he made little effort to investigate violence against the city's African-American citizens. The city even earned the nickname "Bombingham" because of the 18 unsolved bombings there from 1957 to 1963.

On May 2, 1963, more than 1,000 African-American children from the ages of 6 to 18 marched in the streets of Birmingham to protest segregation. More than 950 children were arrested and taken away in school buses. The following day, police blasted the children with high-powered fire hoses and released police dogs on them. Some children were brutally beaten with nightsticks. Photos of the attacks on the peaceful protesters shocked the world and shone a spotlight on civil rights issues in the United States.

Police officers in Birmingham sprayed strong jets of water at protesters to knock them down and keep them from marching.

After the events of Birmingham, the five most important civil rights groups became more open to holding a march in Washington, D.C. Martin Luther King Jr. believed that the march should draw attention to civil rights as well as to economic injustice. As a result, the focus of the march began to change.

The first groups that supported Randolph's proposal were CORE, SNCC, and the SCLC. These three groups were all familiar with the power of nonviolent protest. Members of the groups had been involved in protests throughout the South. James Farmer of CORE, for example, had planned and participated in sit-ins in the 1950s as well as the first Freedom Rides in the 1960s.

SNCC was the youngest of the five groups. John Lewis, head of SNCC, was young, too—just 23 years old—but he was a veteran in the war for equality. He had been jailed for a sit-in in Nashville, Tennessee, and beaten and knocked unconscious at a Freedom Ride in Montgomery, Alabama.

Although Randolph had the support of three groups, he especially needed the NAACP to champion the cause. The NAACP was the oldest group and was one of the most active civil rights organizations in the United States. Starting in the 1930s, it had been successful in challenging segregation and discrimination through the legal and political system. The group's biggest victory was *Brown v. Board of Education,* the court

John Lewis was the youngest of all the march's planners, but he had plenty of experience working for civil rights.

ruling that declared segregation in public schools to be unconstitutional.

Roy Wilkins, head of the NAACP, was not convinced that nonviolent protest was an effective way to win equal rights. In the past, Wilkins had belittled the nonviolent protest methods used by other groups and often said that King's efforts had not integrated a single classroom in the South. He believed that the best way to fight for civil rights was through the U.S. court system. However, Wilkins finally consented to support the march after it was agreed that no laws would be broken.

31

Once Wilkins decided that the NAACP would support the march, Whitney Young Jr., president of the National Urban League, soon agreed. The National Urban League used worker training, education, and counseling to teach African-Americans to be advocates for their own rights and provide them with more opportunities. The group had also been successful in persuading companies to employ more black workers.

As the five civil rights groups were deciding to join the march effort, President Kennedy appeared on television to condemn the events in Birmingham and promise a strong civil rights bill. His appearance on June 11, 1963, marked the first time in U.S. history that a president spoke out publicly against segregation. Kennedy said:

In a televised speech, President Kennedy told Americans that he was sending a civil rights bill to Congress and urged them to support it.

> *One hundred years of delay have passed since President Lincoln freed the slaves, yet their heirs, their grandsons, are not fully free. They are not freed from the bonds of injustice; they are not yet freed from social and economic oppression. And this nation, for all its hopes and boasts, will not be fully free until all its citizens are free. … We preach freedom around the world and we mean it. And we cherish our freedom at home.*

On June 19, Kennedy sent a civil rights bill to Congress. The president's bill, if approved, would put an end to segregation in some public places, including hotels, restaurants, and stores. It would guarantee the right of anyone of legal age with a sixth-grade education to vote. And the bill would give the government the tools needed to end school segregation. Although it was not as strong as some civil rights leaders had hoped, it was a beginning.

Soon after Kennedy announced the civil rights bill, Randolph and the other civil rights leaders decided that the march would also serve as a rally in favor of the president's bill. They knew that the bill faced strong opposition in Congress. Southern politicians had already threatened to hold up any civil rights legislation that came before them.

Together, Randolph and the leaders of each of the civil rights groups became known as the Big Six. They were Roy Wilkins of the NAACP, Whitney Young Jr. of the National Urban League, Martin Luther King Jr. of the SCLC, James Farmer of CORE, and John Lewis of SNCC.

The Big Six met in New York to begin planning the March on Washington (from left): John Lewis, Whitney Young Jr., A. Philip Randolph, Martin Luther King Jr., James Farmer, and Roy Wilkins.

In 1941, Randolph had believed that blacks must march without the help of white people. "We shall not call upon our white friends to march with us," he said. "There are some things Negroes must do alone. This is our fight and we must see it through. ... Let the Negro masses speak!" But this time, white people were welcome to march hand in hand with African-Americans. Membership of the major civil rights groups included both blacks and whites. And in early August 1963, representatives of four groups with white leadership and members were included in the organization of the event. The four new representatives were three religious leaders and a labor organizer. They were Mathew Ahmann of the National Catholic Conference of Interracial Justice; Eugene Carson Blake of the National Council of Churches of Christ in America; Rabbi Joachim Prinz of the American Jewish Congress; and Walter Reuther, president of the United Auto Workers. The Big Six became the Big Ten.

Bayard Rustin was chosen to coordinate the march. Rustin, an associate of both Randolph and King, had a long history in the civil rights struggle. He was also opposed to warfare or any type of violence. As a pacifist, Rustin—like Martin Luther King Jr.—believed that blacks should work for their civil rights through nonviolent protests.

With the March on Washington for Jobs and Freedom planned for August 28, 1963, the group had chosen the right man for the job. Rustin had a clear vision of the march, and he plainly stated its goal: "To embody in one gesture civil rights as well as national economic demands."

PAST PROTESTS

Over the years, Bayard Rustin had become quite an expert at planning boycotts, protests, and other nonviolent actions. During World War II, he spent more than two years in prison because he refused to fight in the war. In 1947, Rustin planned the first Freedom Ride into the South to protest segregation. Eight years later, he helped to plan the Montgomery bus boycott. Rustin had also served as one of the leaders of the Congress of Racial Equality (CORE).

Two Months to Prepare

Chapter

4

When President Kennedy learned of the planned march, he was upset. Kennedy believed that the event would hurt his civil rights bill. Kennedy was also concerned that the march might spark riots and other violence. He and his brother, Attorney General Robert F. Kennedy, met with the Big Six and asked them to call off the event. The president told the men:

> *We want success in Congress, not just a big show at the Capitol. Some of these people are looking for an excuse to be against us. I don't want to give any of them a chance to say, 'Yes, I'm for the bill, but I'm damned if I will vote for it at the point of a gun.' ... The only effect [of the march] is to create an atmosphere of intimidation.*

But the Big Six refused to back down. Randolph told the president that the march would go on. The civil rights leaders left the White House without Kennedy's support.

On July 2, 1963, planning for the March on Washington for Jobs and Freedom began in earnest. That day, the Big Six met at a hotel in New York. Later the same day, they made the first official

Civil rights supporters met with politicians at the White House, including Attorney General Robert F. Kennedy (front row, third from right) and Vice President Lyndon B. Johnson (front row, far right).

announcement that the march would take place. The event's goal, they said, was "to offer a great witness to the basic moral principle of human equality and brotherhood."

With less than two months to prepare, Rustin went to work. He and a crew of about 200 volunteers set up headquarters in a four-story building at West 130th Street in Harlem, a neighborhood in New York City. One of the crew's first acts was to hang a huge banner from the building's third-floor window. The banner read "March on Washington for Jobs and Freedom, August 28, 1963."

During the coming weeks, the headquarters in Harlem would be a place of organized chaos. The building had no elevator and no intercom system. Instead, workers shouted or ran up and down the stairs to communicate with one another. Volunteers staffed desks with telephones and borrowed typewriters, fielding phone calls and giving out information as needed. Workers ate meals together, and some—including Rustin himself—slept at the headquarters on donated cots.

In just two weeks, the workers had created and distributed thousands of copies of an organizing manual to civil rights and other groups. They also began designing, creating, and printing flyers, leaflets, and pamphlets filled with information about the march. Within one month, the group had passed out nearly 400,000 flyers.

Volunteers made thousands of red, white, and blue signs to be carried by marchers. The signs demanded an FEPC, or Fair Employment Practices Committee, law.

One of the crew's chief goals was to raise enough money to pay for the march. The Big Six estimated that they would need about $100,000. The money would be used to pay for portable toilets, drinking fountains, and other supplies. It would also be used to arrange transportation and pay for the pamphlets and other items the volunteers were creating.

Each of the civil rights organizations donated what money it could, but it was still not enough. Rustin reached out to church groups and labor unions, urging them to ask their members to contribute. He also asked celebrities to speak out for the march and hold fund-raisers.

Another way the crew raised money was through the sale of buttons. The buttons showed a black and a white hand clasped together, along with the words "March on Washington for Jobs and Freedom" and the date of the march. Each button was sold for 25 cents. In just one month, organizers sold about 42,000 buttons. The sale of these small buttons earned the group about $15,000 in profit.

Rustin's goal was to attract at least 100,000 marchers. Any less might lead some people to think

March director Bayard Rustin made sure that every part of the event was planned to the last detail, including the route marchers would follow.

that the desire for civil rights was not strong among African-Americans. To make sure that everyone in the United States knew about the march, Rustin held press conferences, gave speeches, and mailed out publicity materials. He spoke on radio and television. He gave newspaper and magazine interviews and appeared at rallies and concerts.

Roy Wilkins played an important role in publicizing the march. Wilkins was one of the best-known civil rights activists in the nation. In April, he had appeared before Congress to talk about the problems African-Americans faced every day. He told the Senate Commerce Committee:

For millions of Americans, this is vacation time. Families load their automobiles and trek across the country. I invite the members of this committee to imagine themselves darker in color and to plan an auto trip from Norfolk, Virginia, to the Gulf Coast of Mississippi. How far would you drive each day? Where and under what conditions can you and your family eat? Where can they use a restroom? Can you stop after a reasonable day behind the wheel, or must you drive until you reach a city where relatives or friends will accommodate you for the night? Will your children be denied an ice-cream cone because they are not white? The Negro American has been waiting upon voluntary action since 1876. He has found what other Americans have discovered: Voluntary action has to be sparked by something stronger than prayers, patience, and lamentation [cries of sorrow].

41

Although he initially hesitated to support the march, Roy Wilkins played a key role in making sure that the event was a success.

Wilkins personally wrote letters to every branch of the NAACP, telling them about the event and asking for their support.

Not all black activists supported the march. Malcolm X, a member of the militant Nation of Islam group, was the most outspoken against the march. Malcolm X believed that the only way blacks could achieve their rights was to fight for them, using violence, when necessary, to protect themselves from whites. The Nation of Islam preached that blacks should take pride in their heritage and live separately from whites in their own black nation. Throughout the coming weeks, Malcolm X would accuse civil rights leaders involved in the march of allowing whites to control the event.

On July 17, nearly a month after meeting with the civil rights leaders, President Kennedy decided to publicly support the march. He also assigned government officials to help Rustin coordinate the event. Kennedy had realized that the march would go on with or without him, and he knew that people around the world would be watching to see how he would handle this peaceful protest against injustice.

To make sure the march remained peaceful, Kennedy asked the Big Six to change the proposed route. He did not want the marchers to pass either the Capitol or the White House. The Big Six responded by rerouting the march. Instead of starting at the Capitol, marchers would make their way from the Washington Monument to the Lincoln Memorial. The speeches and other events would take place entirely on the National Mall. Confining the event to a single area would better enable law enforcement officials to make sure the gathering remained nonviolent.

Once Kennedy came out in support of the march, Rustin sent out invitations to every member of Congress. Few, however, wanted to attend. One Southern Democrat, Senator Olin D. Johnston of South Carolina, replied:

I positively will not attend. You are committing the worst possible mistake in promoting this March. You should know that criminal, fanatical, and communistic elements, as well as crackpots, will move in to take every advantage of this mob. You certainly will have no influence on any members of Congress, especially myself.

On the day of the march, only 50 of 535 members of Congress attended.

As the days before the march ticked by, the excitement and activity at the Harlem headquarters heated up. Volunteers helped make final travel arrangements for people wanting to march. They reminded marchers to bring plenty of water. They asked them to wear comfortable shoes, hats, and sunglasses. They even warned people to avoid bringing sandwiches with mayonnaise because the dressing could go bad on a hot day.

There were problems, too. Anna Arnold Hedgeman was one of the most active and involved members of the march's planning committee. This committee, which helped Rustin and the Big Six coordinate the many details of the march, included other members of the groups that were involved. Hedgeman, the only woman on the committee, was a skilled civil rights activist. She had served as the executive director of President Franklin D. Roosevelt's Fair Employment Practices Committee. Hedgeman had spent her life fighting for the rights of women and African-Americans.

Hedgeman knew that women were the silent heroes of the civil rights movement. They had marched alongside their husbands and brothers, taking the same risks and facing the same dangers. Women had also worked hard behind the scenes, making posters, cooking meals, and doing other important tasks that did not garner much notice. And thousands of women from all over the country planned to attend the march.

A WOMEN'S MARCH

In the early 1900s, women organized their own protest march for equal rights. On March 3, 1913, about 5,000 women paraded from the Capitol to the White House in support of women's right to vote. Black women took part in the march, but they were forced to walk behind white marchers at the parade's end. One black woman, Ida Wells-Barnett, refused to obey the rules and marched with her white friends. Along the parade route, the fighters for women's suffrage were heckled by men shouting at them. Even policemen heckled the marchers and encouraged others to do the same.

Hedgeman was shocked and embarrassed when she learned that women would not be allowed to play a public role in the march events. Male march organizers had decided that no women would speak at the ceremonies. Wives of the Big Six were not allowed to march with their husbands, and no female representative was invited to attend the meeting with President Kennedy after the march. A few key women would be allowed to sit on the podium, but they were the only women allowed to attend. Hedgeman and other female activists were upset.

45

Although she didn't get the credit the male organizers received, Anna Arnold Hedgeman was a driving force behind the march.

At the march committee's final meeting in New York on August 16, Hedgeman read aloud a letter she had sent to Randolph and the other leaders. Although her pleas moved some, they were not enough to persuade the organizers to allow women speakers to be part of the formal march agenda. Instead, the men added a section to the program called "Tribute to Negro Women Fighters for Freedom."

Women who had played key roles in the civil rights struggle would be introduced by Daisy Gatson Bates, a civil rights activist from Little Rock, Arkansas. She would be the only woman invited to speak at the march. ◨

DAISY GATSON BATES

Daisy Gatson Bates of Little Rock, Arkansas, was a newspaper editor and an official for the NAACP. Throughout the crisis at Central High School in 1957, Bates was with the nine students who were trying to attend an all-white school. Throughout their time in the hostile environment, the students knew they could count on Bates for support. Later in life, Bates worked to register voters and end poverty in Washington, D.C. She died in Little Rock in 1999.

Traveling to Washington

Chapter

5

Early on August 25, Rustin, his crew, and most of the Big Ten headed to the nation's capital. Before they left their headquarters in New York, the planners issued a final statement. The march, they promised, "will be orderly but not subservient. It will be proud but not arrogant. It will be nonviolent but not timid."

As the date of the march approached, Rustin's crew in New York City worked around the clock, making sure that everything would be perfect for the big day. More volunteers came forward to help make the event a success. For example, 300 volunteers at the Riverside Church in the city prepared 80,000 cheese sandwiches for hungry marchers. The workers stuffed the sandwiches into brown paper bags, adding apples and slices of marble cake. The lunches were shipped in

Volunteers in New York City made sure that marchers would not go hungry the day of the march.

a refrigerated truck to Washington before the morning of the march.

In the days before the march, the Big Ten and march organizers— including (from left) Mathew Ahmann, Cleveland Robinson, Joachim Prinz, A. Philip Randolph, Joseph Rauh Jr., John Lewis, and Floyd McKissick— traveled to Washington, D.C.

When the leaders arrived in Washington, D.C., they set up headquarters at a local hotel. There the men talked about the upcoming event to the many journalists who had come to interview them. Randolph told the journalists, "No force under the sun can block or stem the civil rights revolution that is on the way."

In Washington, D.C., Rustin attended to last-minute details. He met with National Park Service

employees and talked with nervous police officials. The summer of 1963 had proved to be one of the most violent in many years. There had been numerous clashes. From May 20 to August 10, more than 1,100 civil rights protests had taken place in 220 U.S. cities. During the protests, about 20,000 people had been arrested, and at least 10 people had been killed.

Rustin made plans to keep the march peaceful. He felt it was important that white police officers not be seen lining the march route. So he created his own security force, made up of 2,000 black men dressed in street clothes. Rustin also enlisted the help of 200 male and female ushers from a church ushers' union to keep the event orderly by showing people where to sit and stand. The women dressed in white uniforms; the men wore suits.

EXTRA SECURITY

The White House took steps to ensure that no violence would mar the march. In Washington, D.C., and its surrounding suburbs, police officers who had scheduled to have the day off were ordered to report to work. Firefighters and police reserves were sworn in as temporary officers, and plainclothes police officers were brought in from New York. Two thousand National Guard troops were placed on alert, and soldiers and Marines at nearby bases were ordered to be ready for action. However, police dogs were banned from the march: President Kennedy did not want people to be reminded of events in Birmingham, Alabama.

To reach the march on time, thousands of people set off in cars or buses a day or two before the event. Others started even earlier. On August 15, a group of 12 marchers from CORE's Brooklyn chapter set out from New York on foot. Carrying signs that read "We March from New York City for Freedom," they covered more than 230 miles (368 kilometers) in 13 days. Eighty-two-year-old Jay Hardo rode his bicycle from Dayton, Ohio.

Another man, Ledger Smith, a 27-year-old truck driver and member of the NAACP, roller-skated more than 700 miles (1,120 km) from Chicago to the site of the march. Smith wore a bright red sash with the word *Freedom* written on it. He arrived in Washington after 10 days of roller-skating.

A group of marchers from western Pennsylvania arrived by train on August 28, 1963, to participate in the March on Washington.

People made both large and small sacrifices to attend the march. Some spent their last money on tickets to the nation's capital. Others contributed money to send marchers to Washington, D.C. In Buffalo, New York, a brass company union collected funds so that unemployed workers could be part of the event. In Cleveland, Mississippi, people bought bus tickets for 40 unemployed men who wanted to go on the march.

Early on the morning of Wednesday, August 28, the final wave of marchers set off for the capital. Hundreds of cars and buses hit the roads, heading for the Washington Monument. Special trains, nicknamed "Freedom Trains," chugged out of New York stations. In New York alone, about 55,000 people departed for Washington, D.C., the morning of the march.

For many, the journey to Washington, D.C., was a joyous and uplifting event. Singing songs and talking about the upcoming march, travelers made the time fly. On one train from Chicago, a three-piece jazz band entertained riders. On some routes, travelers looked outside to see supporters lining the road, waving and cheering. Other travelers stopped at churches along the way to enjoy a hot breakfast or a cold snack.

A plane with 30 celebrities departed from Lockheed Airport in Burbank, California. Famous actors and singers who attended the march included Charlton Heston, Marlon Brando,

Lena Horne, Sydney Poitier, Paul Newman, Marian Anderson, and Rita Moreno. These celebrities chose to attend even after receiving phone calls from agents from the Federal Bureau of Investigation (FBI) encouraging them not to take part. Josephine Baker, a famous black dancer who had entertained audiences in the United States and France, made a special trip from Europe to attend the march.

Singer Marian Anderson and actor Paul Newman (right) joined Roy Wilkins of the NAACP at the march.

As marchers arrived in Washington, they found a city that was strangely silent. Many stores and businesses around the city were closed and locked up tight for the day. Workers throughout the city had stayed home that day, hoping to avoid the violence they feared was coming. Bars and liquor stores had been ordered shut, and two major-league baseball games had been postponed. Area hospitals had stockpiled blood supplies and postponed all but emergency surgeries.

CBS News reporter Roger Mudd would later remember people's fears about the march:

> *Washington had never had a march like this. They didn't know what to expect. They expected the worst. They had seen on television the violence, the dogs, the hoses. They hoped it wouldn't happen in Washington, but they didn't know.* ◥

United Against Racism

6

On the morning of August 28, Bayard Rustin rose at daybreak and walked to the National Mall. Everything was peaceful and quiet. By 8 A.M., it was clear that the day would be sunny and beautiful. But Rustin was worried. Only about 50 people so far had gathered near the Washington Monument. And official activities were scheduled to begin in just 90 minutes.

The scene at Washington's Union Station was very different. At 7:30 A.M., the first trains had begun to arrive. They came from Baltimore, Maryland, Jacksonville, Florida, and other cities on the East Coast. They came from Philadelphia and Chicago. The station soon filled with crowds of white and black people, many of them carrying signs, picnic baskets, and lunch bags. Between 9 A.M. and noon, trains pulled into Union Station

Many marchers walked past the Capitol on their way to the National Mall.

every 10 minutes. From there, marchers were taken to the Mall on shuttle buses. Others chose to set out for the Mall on foot. As they walked, they sang freedom songs, spirituals, and gospel tunes such as "We Shall Not Be Moved" and "Ain't Gonna Let Nobody Turn Me 'Round."

By 9:30 A.M., Rustin knew that he had nothing to fear. The crowd at the Washington Monument had increased to about 40,000 people, and by 11 A.M., an estimated 90,000 people had gathered. And they kept coming: Every few minutes, more buses arrived, and shuttles from the train stations dropped off more marchers.

Inside the big striped information tent set up on the Mall, Rustin could survey some of the results of his hard work. As more people arrived, they would have access to 292 outdoor toilets and 21 portable water fountains. Twenty-two first aid stations had been set up, and more than 100 doctors and nurses were ready to treat any ill or injured people.

At the Washington Monument, the day's activities began as scheduled at 9:30 A.M. The early portion of the program was planned to entertain the people before they started marching. Celebrities made brief speeches or recited poetry. Folk singers such as Joan Baez, Odetta, and Bob Dylan performed for the growing crowd. They sang "Oh Freedom," "We Shall Overcome," and "Blowin' in the Wind."

During the morning program, one celebrity who received a warm welcome was Jackie Robinson, the

first African-American major-league baseball player. Robinson, who attended the march with his family, had made his major-league debut with the Brooklyn Dodgers in 1947. Throughout his 10-year career, he suffered the abuse of racist fans, opponents, and even his own teammates.

Within just a few hours, thousands gathered between the Washington Monument and the Lincoln Memorial.

Across from the Mall, George Lincoln Rockwell and about 50 American Nazi Party members glared at the people gathered around the Washington Monument. Rockwell had planned his own march to protest the civil rights demonstration, and it was obvious that he intended to start trouble. He had mailed out pamphlets that said:

> *Over SIX HUNDRED fighting mad white men from Richmond alone have pledged to stand against the nigger terror with us on August 28. … Be in Washington Monument at dawn on August 28 with every single white person— man, woman, and child—you can bring.*

But the National Park Service had turned down his request to hold his march, and now Rockwell could do nothing but watch from across the street, safely behind a line of security guards. When one of the Nazis tried to make a statement, he was promptly arrested for speaking without a permit.

The program at the Washington Monument continued for two hours, but the marchers were getting restless. They hadn't come to be entertained. They had come to march and to hear civil rights leaders speak about their future.

Around 11:20 A.M., groups of people suddenly began the one-mile (1.6-km) march from the Washington Monument to the Lincoln Memorial. Soon, more and more people followed, moving in two streams down Constitution Avenue and Independence Avenue.

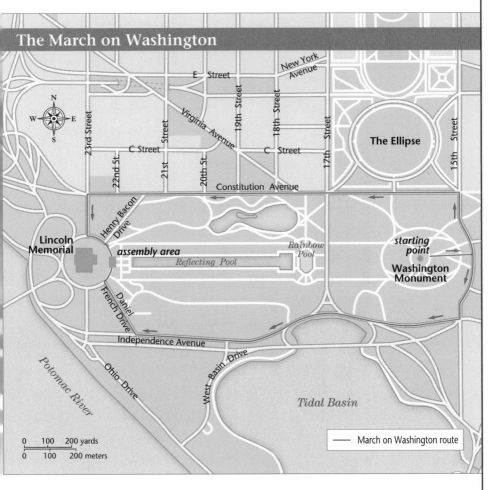

The March on Washington

Scale:
0 100 200 yards
0 100 200 meters

— March on Washington route

Although some of the marchers chanted "Freedom Now" or sang songs as they walked, most were silent. Some wept, and others smiled happily. Many carried the red-and-white or blue-and-white signs they had picked up at the information tent. The signs read "We Demand Equal Rights Now," "We March for Jobs for All Now," and "We March for Integrated Schools Now." Few spectators lined the streets to watch the parade, but one person who did later described the marchers as a "gentle army."

Organizers planned for two parade routes around the National Mall, but many people simply walked directly from the Washington Monument to the Lincoln Memorial.

Marchers carried signs demanding social and economic justice for African-American people in the United States.

Writer Marya Mannes, who attended the march, described the scene:

> *There was ... no attempt at lines, at rhythm, at any formation whatsoever. They did not even stick together except in the loosest way by groups, or states, or organizations, or busloads. They just walked—mostly black, partly white—like people who know where they are going but are not making a show of it. ... A people serious but relaxed; almost festive.*

MARCHING ON WASHINGTON

The March on Washington for Jobs and Freedom was the largest protest in the nation's capital, but it was not the first. On May 1, 1894, businessman Jacob Coxey led a group of about 500 unemployed men down Pennsylvania Avenue to the White House. "Coxey's Army" hoped to persuade Congress to pass laws to aid them. The march ended when Coxey was arrested. He spent 20 days in jail. More than 30 years later, one of the most violent protests in the capital took place during the Great Depression. In 1932, as many as 20,000 World War I veterans flooded Washington, D.C., demanding their "bonus," or payment for service in the U.S. military. Payment wasn't due for another 13 years, but the unemployed veterans wanted their money. Congress refused the pleas of the "Bonus Marchers." Marchers and their families remained in the capital for three months, building shacks or camping out in abandoned buildings. Finally, the U.S. Army chased the former soldiers out of town with tear gas, tanks, and bayonets.

Rustin was caught off guard by the sudden movement of the marchers. He had planned for the Big Ten to lead the marchers to the Lincoln Memorial. However, the leaders were still at Capitol Hill, meeting with members of Congress. When the men were told that the march had begun, they quickly left the Capitol. Rustin found a gap in the parade of marchers and placed the leaders at the front. The men linked arms, and the photographers' pictures made it look as if they were at the head of the march, not in the middle. ◨

We Shall Overcome

Chapter

7

By noon on August 28, about 250,000 people had gathered on the National Mall between the two memorials. On this sunny, late-summer day, temperatures were already climbing into the low 80s Fahrenheit (mid-20s Celsius). The gathering took in a picniclike atmosphere, with people sitting on the grass eating sack lunches. Others soaked their feet in the Mall's Reflecting Pool or sought the shade of trees on the Mall. Food stands and ice-cream carts provided marchers with a cold soda or frozen treat.

As the crowd packed closer together, the heat began to take a toll. Some people fainted and were treated by medics. But still the marchers remained polite and orderly, with people of all races, religions, and backgrounds waiting patiently together in anticipation.

Thousands of people crowded together along the National Mall, waiting to hear the speeches of civil rights activists.

John Lewis of SNCC described the scene:

> *You saw black and white, Protestant, Catholic and Jewish, old and young, rich and poor. ... You saw black and white feet dipped in the Reflecting Pool. You could feel the great sense of community and family. The March on Washington represented America at her best.*

Although the day had been peaceful, government officials were ready to act if things changed. A White House official sat near the podium, ready to cut the power to the sound system if any speaker tried to incite violence or rebellion. Direct phone lines were hooked up between government observation posts and the Pentagon. Plainclothes officers from the Secret Service also mixed into the crowd. And FBI agents were stationed on top of both the Washington Monument and the Lincoln Memorial. Some marchers sensed the tension and fear. One woman, 35-year-old Nettie Hailes, recalled closing her eyes and praying for the event to end peacefully.

Whatever happened, people around the world would be watching. The March on Washington received media coverage unlike any other event. Even the inauguration of President Kennedy had not received such attention. All three major television networks covered the march. CBS had its cameras rolling throughout the official program, from 1:30 to 4:30 P.M. NBC and ABC broke into their regularly scheduled programming to broadcast King's speech.

More than 2,000 journalists from the United States and other countries reported on the march.

At 2 P.M., the official program began. Opera singer Marian Anderson, scheduled to sing the national anthem, was stuck in the crowd and was unable to get to the platform in time. Opera singer Camilla Williams from Virginia did the honors instead. Anderson would later sing "He's Got the Whole World in His Hands."

Over the next three hours, the audience would listen as each member of the Big Ten—plus Daisy Gatson Bates, the lone woman—vowed to continue the fight for civil rights. One of the first people to speak was A. Philip Randolph, the march's mastermind and master of ceremonies. Randolph told the crowd:

> ### MARIAN ANDERSON AND THE LINCOLN MEMORIAL
>
> For Marian Anderson, singing at the Lincoln Memorial in 1963 brought back memories of a concert there more than 20 years earlier. In 1939, the Daughters of the American Revolution had barred Anderson from performing at Constitution Hall in Washington, D.C., because of her race. When First Lady Eleanor Roosevelt heard of the group's action, she was furious. Roosevelt resigned as a member of the group and made arrangements for Anderson to sing at the Lincoln Memorial instead. On April 9, 1939, more than 75,000 people came to the memorial to hear the singer's performance.

We here, today, are only the first wave. When we leave, it will be to carry the civil rights revolution home with us into every nook and cranny of the land. And we shall return again and again to Washington in ever-growing numbers until total freedom is ours.

67

Early in the program, Bates stepped up to the microphone to present the march's "Tribute to Negro Women Fighters for Freedom." Bates told the crowd about some of the women who had played a key role in the civil rights struggle. These women were Diane Nash Bevel, Gloria Richardson, Myrlie Evers, Prince Estella Lee, and the mother of the movement, Rosa Parks. Bevel and Richardson had both led demonstrations and protests against discrimination and segregation. Evers and Lee were the widows of NAACP members who had been assassinated by segregationists in the South. Only Evers, who was attending an event in Boston, was

Civil rights activist Daisy Gatson Bates was the only woman allowed to speak from the podium during the march ceremonies.

unable to be at the march. Bates finished the tribute with the following words:

> *We will kneel-in, we will sit-in, until we can eat in any counter in the United States. We will walk until we are free, until we can walk to any school and take our children to any school in the United States.*

After the women's tribute, John Lewis, chairman of SNCC, moved to the microphone. Twenty-three-year-old Lewis, the youngest speaker at the march, was also the most controversial. His proposed speech had already caused a serious rift behind the scenes. Lewis' original speech had begun with some fiery words for President Kennedy. He wrote, "In good conscience, we cannot support the administration's civil rights bill, for it is too little, and too late." The rest of the speech had included parts that some people felt might encourage violence or rebellion. He wrote:

> *The revolution is at hand and we must free ourselves of the chains of political and economic slavery. ... We will march through the South, through the heart of Dixie ... leaving a scorched earth with our nonviolence.*

However, when Archbishop Patrick O'Boyle learned of the contents of Lewis' speech, he threatened to refuse to say the opening prayer. To avoid the bad publicity, Rustin asked Lewis and the other SNCC members to rewrite the address. At first, Lewis refused. Then Randolph stepped in, saying that he had waited 22 years for this moment, and asked the young men to change the speech.

Lewis and the others finally agreed to rewrite the speech, toning down the most controversial parts. However, the 10-minute-long talk was still the most radical of the day. The young man told his listeners:

> To those who say 'be patient and wait,' we must say that we cannot be patient. We do not want our freedom gradually, but we want to be free now. We are tired. ... How long can we be patient? We want our freedom and we want it now.

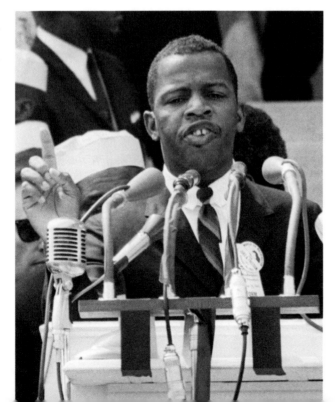

John Lewis, the youngest of the Big Ten, gave the most controversial speech of the day.

Lewis encouraged listeners to "get in and stay in the streets of every city, every village and hamlet of this nation until true freedom comes, until the revolution of 1776 is complete."

When Lewis was finished, all of the African-Americans on the stage rose to shake his hand. The white men, however, stayed seated, refusing to smile or acknowledge the speaker. The next day, *The New York Times* did not include an excerpt of Lewis' speech in its article on the march.

After Lewis spoke, labor leader Walter P. Reuther took President Kennedy to task for paying more attention to foreign affairs than to problems at home. He said:

> *I am for civil rights and equal opportunity because freedom is an invincible value and so long as any person is denied his freedom, my freedom is in jeopardy. I am for civil rights and equal opportunity because American democracy cannot defend freedom in Berlin as long as we continue to deny freedom in Birmingham.*

One of the Big Ten was unable to attend the march. James Farmer, founder of CORE, was sitting in jail in Louisiana. He had been arrested for disturbing the peace by trying to organize protests in the town of Plaquemine. Farmer sent a message, which was read by his colleague Floyd McKissick:

> We [Farmer and 233 other jailed freedom
> fighters] cannot be with you in body, but
> we are with you in spirit. By marching on
> Washington, your tramping feet have spoken
> the message of our struggle in Louisiana—you
> have given voice to the struggle of our people
> in Mississippi and Alabama, too, and in
> California and Chicago and New York. You
> have come from all over the nation and in one
> mighty voice you have spoken to the nation.

The day's program was half over when Whitney
Young Jr. of the National Urban League took the
microphone. Young focused on the poor conditions
under which African-Americans lived:

> They [African-Americans] must march from
> the rat-infested, overcrowded ghettos to
> decent, wholesome, unrestricted residential
> areas dispersed throughout our cities. They
> must march from our cemeteries, where our
> young, our newborn die three times sooner and
> our parents die seven years earlier. ... They
> must march from the congested, ill-equipped
> schools that breed dropouts and which
> smother motivation to the well-equipped,
> integrated facilities throughout the cities. And
> finally they must march from a present feeling
> of hopelessness, despair, and frustration to a
> renewed faith and confidence due to tangible
> programs and visible changes made possible
> only by walking together.

Many marchers had looked forward to the
appearance of Roy Wilkins, head of the NAACP.
Randolph introduced him as the leader of the

nation's civil rights movement. Many were surprised when Wilkins criticized Kennedy's civil rights bill as being weak. He also mocked the government for not doing more to stop violence against blacks:

> Now, my friends, all over this land, and especially in the Deep South, we are beaten and kicked and maltreated and shot and killed by local and state law enforcement officers. It is simply incomprehensible to us here today and to millions of others far from this spot that the United States government, which can regulate the contents of a pill, apparently is powerless to prevent the physical abuse of citizens within its own borders.

Although he criticized President Kennedy's civil rights bill as being weak, Roy Wilkins urged politicians to pass it.

As the day wore on, many in the crowd were becoming restless. Some had already left the Mall, and others were packing up and preparing to leave. Then Mahalia Jackson took the stage and sang two gospel songs. Her powerful voice rang through the crowd, providing a burst of energy to all who heard her.

Joachim Prinz of the American Jewish Congress reminded all Americans what had happened when Germans remained silent in the face of Nazi oppression. During World War II, 6 million Jewish men, women, and children were murdered by the Nazis. Prinz warned the listeners:

Mahalia Jackson, known as the "Queen of Gospel Song," was famous around the world for singing religious songs.

America must not become a nation of onlookers. It must not be silent. Not merely black America, but all of America. It must speak up and act, from the president down to the humblest of us, and not for the sake of the colored citizens but for the sake of America.

Finally Randolph introduced the man whom many marchers had come to hear—Martin Luther King Jr. He had become one of the best-known civil rights activists after helping to lead the Montgomery bus boycott in 1955 and then organizing the highly publicized civil rights protests in Birmingham in 1963. Now Randolph introduced King as the moral leader of the nation. People stood to hear what the most famous civil rights leader would say.

King told listeners that when writing the Declaration of Independence and the U.S. Constitution, the Founding Fathers of the United States had promised all Americans—black and white alike—life, liberty, and the pursuit of happiness. He told marchers that they had come to Washington to cash a check, "a check that will give us upon demand the riches of freedom and the security of justice." And he warned Americans "we will not be satisfied until justice rolls down like water and righteousness like a mighty stream."

As the preacher from Alabama spoke of his dreams for the future, the whole world became his congregation. Some people wept and cheered; others were stunned into silence. The address would become the most famous of the march, and one of King's best-known speeches. King ended with words from an old spiritual song that many blacks knew by heart: "Free at last! Free at last! Thank God almighty, we are free at last!"

After King sat down, Rustin read out a list of the demands of the march. They included the passage of Kennedy's civil rights bill, an end to housing discrimination, programs to ease unemployment, and immediate desegregation. After each demand, members of the crowd roared their approval.

The audience reacted to King's powerful speech with applause and joy.

The last speaker of the day was A. Philip Randolph, the father of the march. He asked the marchers to take a pledge to carry the message of the march back to their friends and neighbors:

> *I pledge to carry the message of the march to my friends and neighbors back home and to arouse them to an equal commitment and an equal effort. I will march and I will write letters. I will demonstrate and I will vote. I will work and make sure that my voice and those of my brothers ring clear and determined from every corner of our land.*

At 4:30 P.M., the marchers packed up their belongings and left the Mall. The march had been more successful than any of its organizers had ever imagined. As Randolph silently watched the marchers leave, Rustin joined him. Randolph told his friend that the march was "the most beautiful and glorious day of my life." Remembered Rustin, "To see this giant with tears in his eyes moved me to want to do everything I humanly could do to bring about justice, not only for black people but for whoever is in trouble."

Soon after the march ended, the Big Ten were driven to the White House to meet with President Kennedy. The president congratulated the men and offered them coffee, sandwiches, and cherry cobbler. Although their discussion lasted an hour, Kennedy made no promises to the Big Ten about civil rights or desegregation. ▲

Legacy of a March

Chapter

8

The March on Washington for Jobs and Freedom left a lasting impression on those who witnessed it—whether in person or on television. The march brought the economic and social injustices faced by African-Americans out into the open for millions to see. It forced Americans to face the reality that they lived in a nation where a person's skin color often determined the quality of his or her life.

The March on Washington showed that African-Americans wanted things to change. It showed that they would stand together and demand the rights they had been promised a century before. The march also underlined the fact that black and white people could work peacefully together for change. Civil rights activists were re-energized by the march. When

The March on Washington brought a renewed sense of purpose to the activists—black and white—who fought for social change.

they returned to the segregated South, most were fired up and ready to fight harder than ever.

The march didn't change things overnight. Polls taken shortly after the event showed that most white Southerners opposed Kennedy's civil rights bill. And the violence in the South continued. Just two weeks after the March on Washington, a bomb was planted by the Ku Klux Klan in the 16th Street Baptist Church in Birmingham, Alabama. The bombing resulted in the deaths of four girls who were changing into their choir robes in the church basement.

In November 1963, a few months after the Birmingham bombings, John F. Kennedy was killed by an assassin's bullet. But his civil rights bill lived on, and within a year it passed. On July 2, 1964, Lyndon B. Johnson—who had become president after Kennedy's assassination—signed the Civil Rights Act of 1964 into law. King and other civil rights leaders proudly watched the historic signing. They had fought hard for this moment.

The act banned discrimination in such public places as theaters, hotels, restaurants, and gas

THE 16TH STREET BAPTIST CHURCH

In the 1950s and 1960s, the 16th Street Baptist Church in Birmingham, Alabama, was more than just a house of worship. The church also served as a center for the city's civil rights movement. Martin Luther King Jr. often spoke there. In May 1963, the church was the stepping-off point for hundreds of children who marched against segregation. In 2006, it was made a National Historic Landmark. Today it remains open for visitors and worshippers alike.

stations. It banned discrimination by employers or labor unions with 100 or more members. And it gave the attorney general the power to end segregation in other places, including schools, hospitals, and libraries. To make sure that people obeyed, the bill gave the U.S. government the power to cancel federally funded programs if communities and states did not comply.

Mourners gathered to say goodbye to 14-year-old Carol Robertson, one of the four children killed in a bombing just weeks after the March on Washington.

81

President Lyndon B. Johnson signed the Civil Rights Act into law in July 1964. The following year, he signed the Voting Rights Act into law.

The following year, Johnson signed the Voting Rights Act into law. That law, as important as the Civil Rights Act, prohibited states from using literacy tests to prevent people from voting. The law allowed greater government regulation in areas where blacks had been prevented from voting.

And it allowed the attorney general to challenge the legality of poll taxes, charges used to prevent poor people from voting.

The struggle for civil rights did not end after the passage of these laws, however. Inequality and discrimination continue to be serious problems in the United States today. In the years after the march, some activists became impatient with the slow pace of change. As a result, groups such as SNCC and CORE became more militant over time.

In the years after the march, the Big Six continued to fight for social justice and equality. In 1965, Randolph formed the A. Philip Randolph Institute, an organization to research and fight poverty. Bayard Rustin headed the organization until 1979. Roy Wilkins of the NAACP and Whitney Young Jr. of the Urban League also remained active in civil rights causes until their deaths.

Martin Luther King Jr. continued to speak out against injustice. The year after the march, he was awarded the Nobel Peace Prize for his efforts. King's life was cut short on April 4, 1968, by an assassin's bullet in Memphis, Tennessee. In 1986, Congress created a national holiday to honor his work.

James Farmer of CORE and John Lewis of SNCC became involved in government. Farmer served as President Richard M. Nixon's assistant secretary of health, education, and welfare in 1969 and 1970. In 1986, Lewis was elected a U.S. representative from Georgia and has served in Congress ever since.

On October 16, 1995, more than 800,000 black men attended the Million Man March in Washington, D.C. The goal of the march, which was organized by Nation of Islam leader Louis Farrakhan, was to encourage black men to take a more active role in their communities. The march also served as a protest against recent political measures that were seen as harmful to minorities and the poor. In the months following the march, 1.5 million black men registered to vote.

In 2003, a rally was held in front of the Lincoln Memorial to mark the 40th anniversary of the March on Washington. Coretta Scott King, widow of Martin Luther King Jr., spoke at the rally, reminding people that the work the Big Six had started was not yet finished:

We have not overcome yet. It is true that we have made great progress in many areas. ... Yet we have a long way to go before we realize Martin's dream of a nation united in justice, equality, and peace. Despite the impressive gains of the last four decades, African-Americans are underrepresented in the U.S. Congress, state legislatures, county commissions, and city councils. Nor have we achieved parity of economic opportunity. ... Racial discrimination and other forms of bigotry remain tenacious evils in our society. Poverty and social injustice still grind the hope out of millions of lives. War and violence continue to afflict our world with increasing brutality and destruction. But I think we have cause for hope. ... If we keep faith with

Martin's teachings and join together with an energized recommitment to create the beloved community, we will one day be celebrating his vision as a glorious reality.

John Lewis
(second from left)
and Coretta Scott
King (center)
gathered with
hundreds of
other people to
commemorate the
40th anniversary
of the historic
March on
Washington.

John Lewis, the only living member of the Big Six, attended and told listeners of the impact that people working together for justice can have. He said, "Because of the March on Washington 40 years ago, we did not just change our nation, we changed the world."

Timeline

January 1863

President Abraham Lincoln issues the Emancipation Proclamation.

December 6, 1865

The 13th Amendment to the U.S. Constitution is ratified.

February 12, 1909

The National Association for the Advancement of Colored People (NAACP) is formed.

September 29, 1910

The Committee on Urban Conditions Among Negroes is formed; the group will later evolve into the National Urban League.

March 3, 1913

About 5,000 women march in Washington, D.C., in support of women's right to vote.

May–July 1932

World War I veterans known as "Bonus Marchers" demonstrate in Washington, D.C., to demand payment for their wartime services.

January 15, 1941

 A. Philip Randolph announces a march on Washington to protest racist hiring policies in U.S. defense industries; he later calls it off.

1942

Students in Chicago found the Congress of Racial Equality (CORE) to fight racism and discrimination.

May 17, 1954

The Supreme Court rules that segregation in public schools is unconstitutional in *Brown v. Board of Education.*

December 1, 1955

 Rosa Parks refuses to give up her seat on a Montgomery, Alabama, bus to a white man, sparking the modern civil rights movement.

January 12, 1957

The Southern Christian Leadership Conference (SCLC) is founded in Atlanta, Georgia.

September 25, 1957

Nine black students begin attending Central High School in Little Rock, Arkansas, despite the efforts of segregationists to stop them.

1960

Senator John F. Kennedy promises that he will end segregation if he is elected president.

April 15–17, 1960

College students in Raleigh, North Carolina, found the Student Nonviolent Coordinating Committee (SNCC).

December 1962

Randolph revives his plans to organize a jobs march on Washington.

March 1963

Randolph sends his proposal for a march to the major civil rights groups in the United States.

Spring 1963

An estimated 75,000 Americans take part in civil rights demonstrations during a one-month period.

May 3, 1963

Police in Birmingham, Alabama, set police dogs on children taking part in a civil rights protest; the children are also beaten with nightsticks and blasted with fire hoses.

June 11, 1963

President Kennedy speaks out against segregation and violence against black people; he promises to send a strong civil rights bill to Congress.

June 19, 1963

Kennedy sends his civil rights bill to Congress.

June 22, 1963

 Kennedy invites the Big Six to the White House and asks them to call off the march.

July 2, 1963

The Big Six hold their first official meeting.

July 17, 1963

President Kennedy agrees to publicly support the march.

Summer 1963

March organizers set up headquarters in Harlem, New York, to prepare for the event; the Big Ten publicize the march through letters, interviews, and TV appearances.

August 16, 1963

At the planning committee's final meeting in New York, Anna Arnold Hedgeman asks the men to allow women to speak.

August 25, 1963

Bayard Rustin heads to Washington, D.C., to make final preparations.

August 28, 1963

7:30 A.M.

Trains carrying marchers begin pulling into Washington, D.C.'s Union Station.

8 A.M.

People slowly begin arriving at the Washington Monument for the March on Washington.

Timeline

9:30 A.M.

March activities begin at the Washington Monument; folk singers and celebrities perform for the crowd.

11:00 A.M.

An estimated 90,000 marchers have arrived at the Washington Monument.

11:20 A.M.

People begin the march to the Lincoln Memorial.

NOON

An estimated 250,000 marchers have gathered on the Mall.

2 P.M.

The afternoon portion of the program kicks off with the singing of "The Star-Spangled Banner."

4:30 P.M.

The March on Washington ends, and the Big Ten leave to meet with President Kennedy.

September 15, 1963

A bombing in Birmingham, Alabama, takes the lives of four girls attending Sunday school.

July 2, 1964

President Lyndon B. Johnson signs the Civil Rights Act into law.

August 6, 1965

President Johnson signs the Voting Rights Act into law.

April 4, 1968

Martin Luther King Jr. is assassinated in Memphis, Tennessee.

October 16, 1995

More than 800,000 black men attend the Million Man March to show their unity and commitment to improving their lives and communities.

August 25, 2003

Civil rights activists commemorate the 40th anniversary of the March on Washington for Jobs and Freedom.

On the Web

For more information on this topic, use FactHound.

1 Go to *www.facthound.com*

2 Type in this book ID: 0756533392

3 Click on the *Fetch It!* button. FactHound will find the best Web sites for you.

Historic Sites

Lincoln Memorial
West Potomac Park
23rd Street N.W.
Washington, DC 20024
202/426-6841

The monument to the Great Emancipator was the site of Martin Luther King Jr.'s historic "I Have a Dream" speech.

A. Philip Randolph Pullman Porter Museum
10406 S. Maryland Ave.
Chicago, IL 60628
773/928-3935

Visitors can learn more about the civil rights pioneer's early career and union work.

Look For More Books in This Series

The Berlin Wall:
Barrier to Freedom

Black Tuesday:
Prelude to the Great Depression

A Day Without Immigrants:
Rallying Behind America's Newcomers

Freedom Rides:
Campaign for Equality

The National Grape Boycott:
A Victory for Farmworkers

The Teapot Dome Scandal:
Corruption Rocks 1920s America

Third Parties:
Influential Political Alternatives

A complete list of **Snapshots in History** titles is available on our Web site: *www.compasspointbooks.com*

Glossary

activist
a person who actively fights for a cause

advocate
a person who supports a cause

bigotry
beliefs and actions that show hatred of those who are different

Big Six
group made up of march organizer A. Philip Randolph and the leaders of the five major civil rights groups

Big Ten
group made up of the Big Six and four white leaders of other organizations

boycott
to stop buying or using something as a form of protest

CORE
abbreviation for the Congress of Racial Equality, a civil rights organization founded in 1942; a member of the Big Six, it was led in 1963 by James Farmer

discrimination
the act of treating one group of people unfairly, often because of race

integrated
open to people of all races

NAACP
abbreviation for the National Association for the Advancement of Colored People, a civil rights organization founded in 1909; a member of the Big Six, it was led in 1963 by Roy Wilkins

National Urban League
organization founded in 1910 to aid African-Americans who had moved to New York City from the South; a member of the Big Six, it was led in 1963 by Whitney Young Jr.

racism
the belief that one race is better than others

SCLC
abbreviation for the Southern Christian Leadership Conference, a civil rights organization founded in 1957; a member of the Big Six, it was co-founded by Martin Luther King Jr. and was led by him until his death

segregation
the separation of a group of people from the rest of society based on race

SNCC
abbreviation for the Student Nonviolent Coordinating Committee, a civil rights organization founded in 1960; a member of the Big Six, it was led in 1963 by John Lewis

social justice
equality and fairness for all people in a society

subservient
willing to do what others demand

suffrage
the right to vote

Chapter 1
Page 12, lines 5, 18, and 22: Martin Luther King Jr. "I Have a Dream Speech, August 28, 1963." *The New York Times.* 29 Aug. 1963, p. 21.

Page 13, line 7: Ibid.

Page 14, line 8: Ibid.

Page 15, line 14: Peter Jennings. "I Have a Dream." ABC News. 28 Aug. 2003. 11 Dec. 2006. http://abcnews.go.com/WNT/story?id=129482

Chapter 2
Page 20, line 22: Patrik Henry Bass. *Like a Mighty Stream: The March on Washington, August 28, 1963.* Philadelphia: Running Press Book Publishers, 2002, p. 48.

Page 21, line 23: Clayborne Carson, David J. Garrow, Gerald Gill, Vincent Harding, and Darlene Clark Hine, eds. *The Eyes on the Prize Civil Rights Reader.* New York: Penguin Books, 1991, p. 92.

Chapter 3
Page 33, line 1: John F. Kennedy. "Radio and Television Report, June 11, 1963." 11 June 1963. John F. Kennedy Presidential Library and Museum. 8 Dec. 2006. www.jfklibrary.org/Historical+Resources/Archives/Reference+Desk/Speeches/JFK/003POF03CivilRights06111963.htm.

Page 34, line 2: Herbert Garfinkel. *When Negroes March.* New York: Atheneum, 1969, Preface.

Page 35, line 24: Steven Kasher. "The March on Washington, 1963." *The Civil Rights Movement: A Photographic History, 1954–68* (excerpt). Abbeville.com. 5 March 2007. www.abbeville.com/civilrights/washington.asp

Chapter 4
Page 36, line 9: Jonathan Rosenberg and Zachary Karabell. *Kennedy, Johnson, and the Quest for Justice.* New York: W.W. Norton & Company, Inc., 2003, p. 130.

Page 38, line 2: Lucy G. Barber. *Marching on Washington: The Forging of an American Political Tradition.* Berkeley: University of California Press, 2002, p. 148.

Page 41, line 14: *Like a Mighty Stream,* p. 92.

Page 44, line 1: Ibid., p. 95.

Chapter 5
Page 48, line 5, and Page 50, line 7: John D'Emilio. *Lost Prophet: The Life and Times of Bayard Rustin.* New York: Free Press, 2003, p. 352.

Page 55, line 13: "I Have a Dream."

Chapter 6
Page 60, line 8: Drew D. Hanson. *The Dream: Martin Luther King, Jr. and the Speech that Inspired a Nation.* New York: HarperCollins, 2003, p. 38.

Page 61, line 11: Russell Baker. "Capital is Occupied by a Gentle Army." *The New York Times.* 29 Aug. 1963.

Source Notes

Page 62, line 3: Sean Dennis Cashman. *African Americans and the Quest for Civil Rights, 1900–1990*. New York: New York University Press, 1991, p. 165.

Chapter 7

Page 66, line 2: Coretta Scott King. "Forty Years Later ... Have We Overcome Yet?" *Ebony.* August 2003, p. 164.

Page 67, line 25: *Like a Mighty Stream,* pp. 125–126.

Page 69, line 3: Daisy Bates. "Address at March on Washington, August 28, 1963." *The New York Times.* 29 Aug. 1963, p. 21.

Page 69, line 15: *African Americans and the Quest for Civil Rights, 1900–1990,* p. 164.

Page 69, line 20: Henry Hampton and Steve Fayer with Sarah Flynn. *Voices of Freedom.* New York: Bantam, 1990, p. 166.

Page 70, line 10: Sanford Wexler. *The Civil Rights Movement: An Eyewitness History.* New York: Facts on File, 1993, p. 187.

Page 71, line 1: *Lost Prophet: The Life and Times of Bayard Rustin,* p. 355.

Page 71, line 15: *The Civil Rights Movement: An Eyewitness History,* p. 187.

Page 72, line 1: Ibid.

Page 72, line 15: Whitney Young Jr. "Speech at the March on Washington, August 28, 1963." *The New York Times.* 29 Aug. 1963, p. 21.

Page 73, line 6: Roy Wilkins. "Speech at the March on Washington, August 28, 1963." *The New York Times.* 29 Aug. 1963, p. 21.

Page 75, line 1: *The Civil Rights Movement: An Eyewitness History,* p. 188.

Page 75, line 22: *The Dream: Martin Luther King, Jr. and the Speech that Inspired a Nation,* p. 53.

Page 75, line 24: "I Have a Dream Speech, August 28, 1963."

Page 77, line 5: *Like a Mighty Stream,* p. 136.

Page 77, line 18: Ibid., p. 137.

Page 77, line 20: *Voices of Freedom,* pp. 169–170.

Chapter 8

Page 84, line 17: "Forty Years Later ... Have We Overcome Yet?"

Page 85, line 8: David Pitts. "The 40th Anniversary of the March on Washington for Jobs and Freedom—Have We Fulfilled the Dream?" 25 Aug. 2003. U.S. Department of State: International Information Programs. 11 Dec. 2006. http://usinfo.state.gov/usa/civilrights/anniversary/

SELECT BIBLIOGRAPHY

Barber, Lucy G. *Marching on Washington: The Forging of an American Political Tradition.* Berkeley: University of California Press, 2002.

Bass, Patrik Henry. *Like a Mighty Stream: The March on Washington, August 28, 1963.* Philadelphia: Running Press Book Publishers, 2002.

Branch, Taylor. *Pillar of Fire: America in the King Years, 1963–1965.* New York: Simon & Schuster, 1998.

Cashman, Sean Dennis. *African-Americans and the Quest for Civil Rights, 1900–1990.* New York: New York University Press, 1991.

D'Emilio, John. *Lost Prophet: The Life and Times of Bayard Rustin.* New York: Free Press, 2003.

Garfinkel, Herbert. *When Negroes March.* New York: Atheneum, 1969.

Hampton, Henry, and Steve Fayer with Sarah Flynn. *Voices of Freedom.* New York: Bantam, 1990.

Hanson, Drew D. *The Dream: Martin Luther King, Jr. and the Speech that Inspired a Nation.* New York: HarperCollins, 2003.

Pfeffer, Paula F. *A. Philip Randolph, Pioneer of the Civil Rights Movement.* Baton Rouge: Louisiana State University Press, 1990.

FURTHER READING

Andryzewski, Tricia. *March on Washington, 1963: Gathering to Be Heard.* Brookfield, Conn.: Millbrook Press, 1996.

Finlayson, Reggie. *We Shall Overcome: The History of the American Civil Rights Movement.* Minneapolis: Lerner Publications Company, 2002.

King, Martin Luther, Jr. *I Have a Dream.* San Francisco: Harper, 1993.

Miller, Calvin Craig. *No Easy Answers: Bayard Rustin and the Civil Rights Movement.* Greensboro, N.C.: Morgan Reynolds Publishing, 2005.

Rappaport, Doreen. *Nobody Gonna Turn Me 'Round: Stories and Songs of the Civil Rights Movement.* Cambridge, Mass.: Candlewick Press, 2006.

Index

ABOUT THE AUTHOR

Robin S. Doak is a writer and former editor of *Weekly Reader* and *U*S*Kids magazine*. She has written many nonfiction books for children. She lives with her husband, two children, two dogs, and two cats in central Connecticut.

IMAGE CREDITS